ULTIMATE
ANIMALS
COLORING BOOK

This Book
Belongs To

Color Swatch
Test your color here !

Before beginning to color, please place a blank page behind each one,
to prevent bleed-trough to the next page.

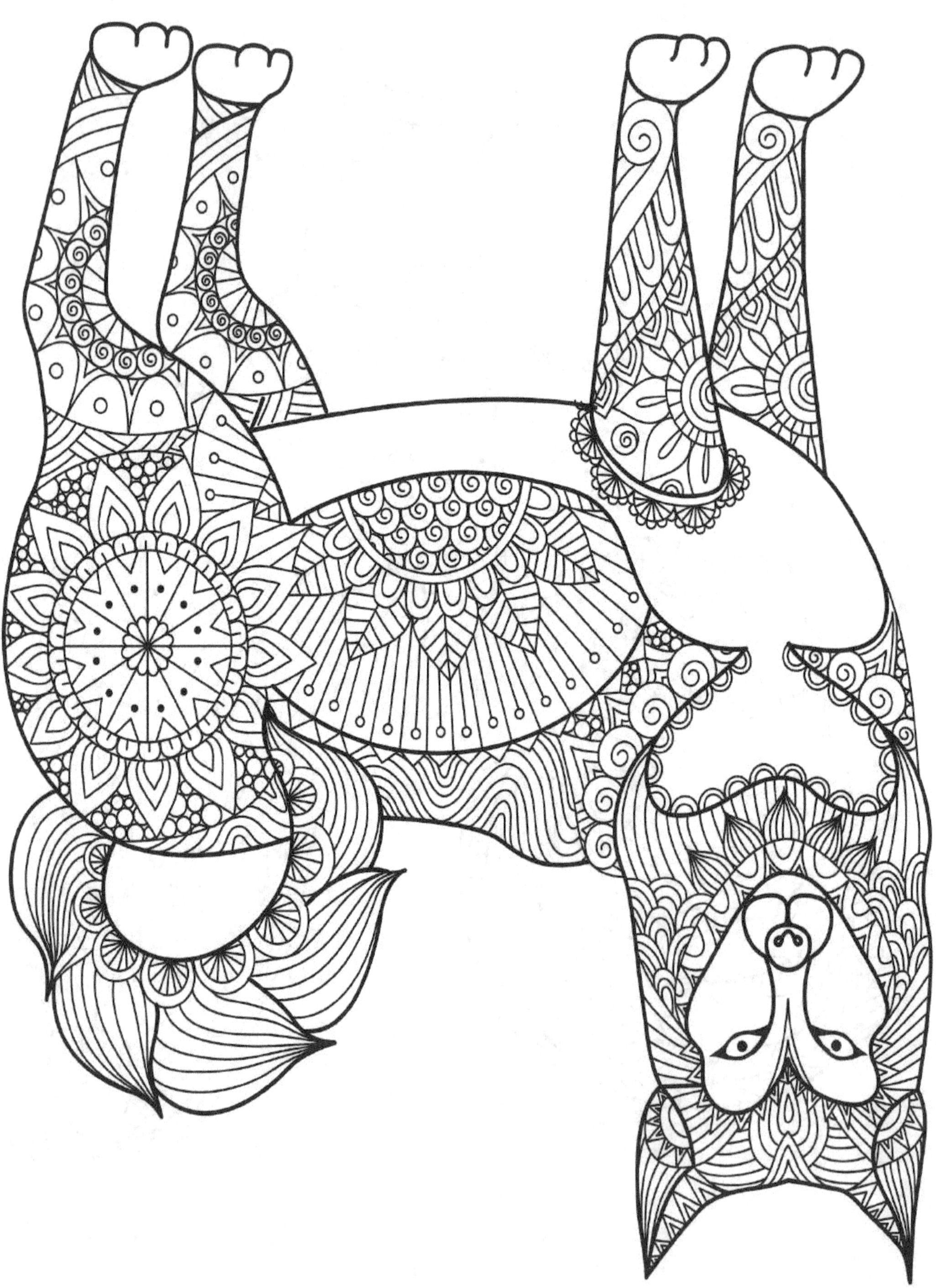

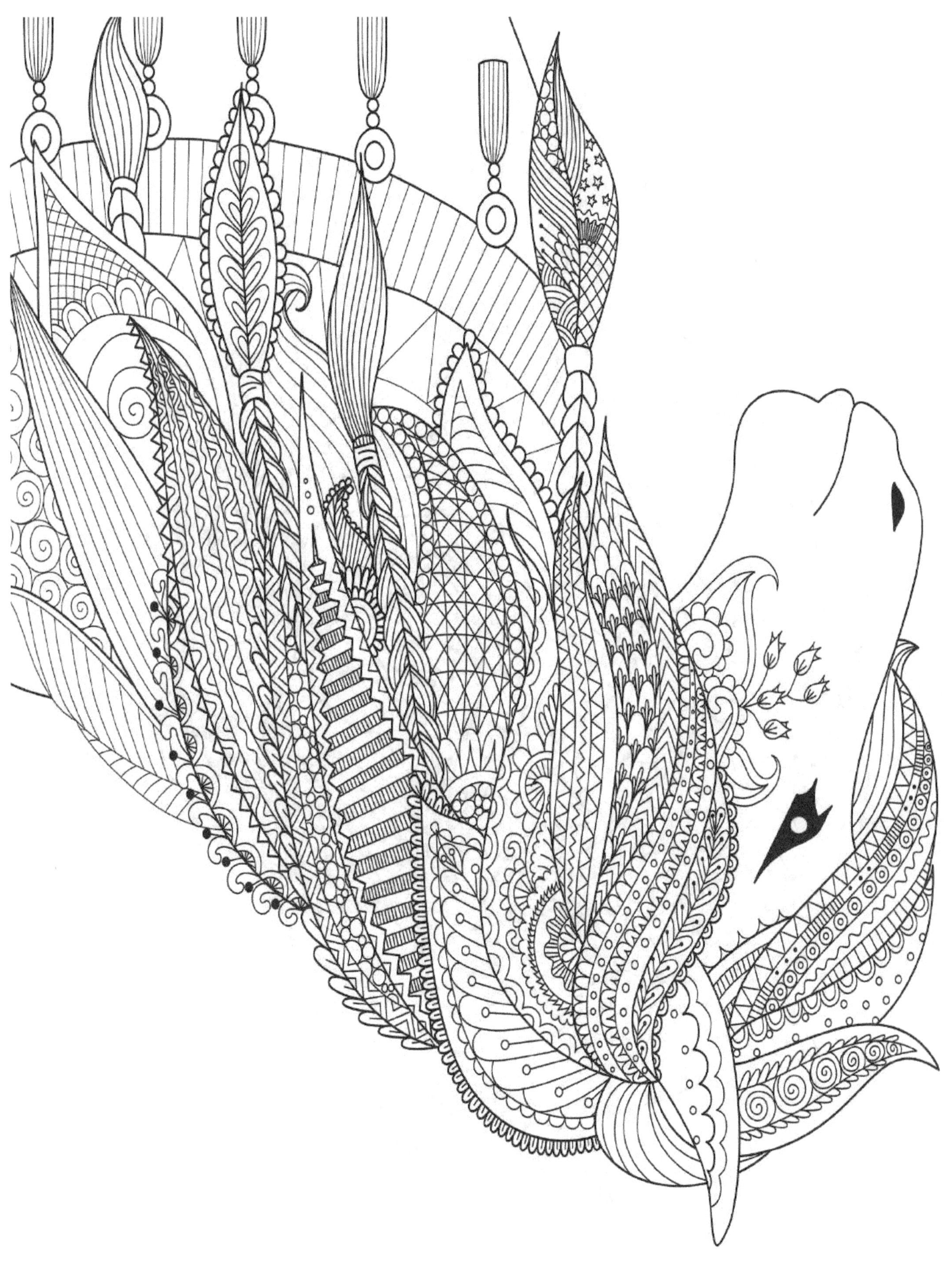

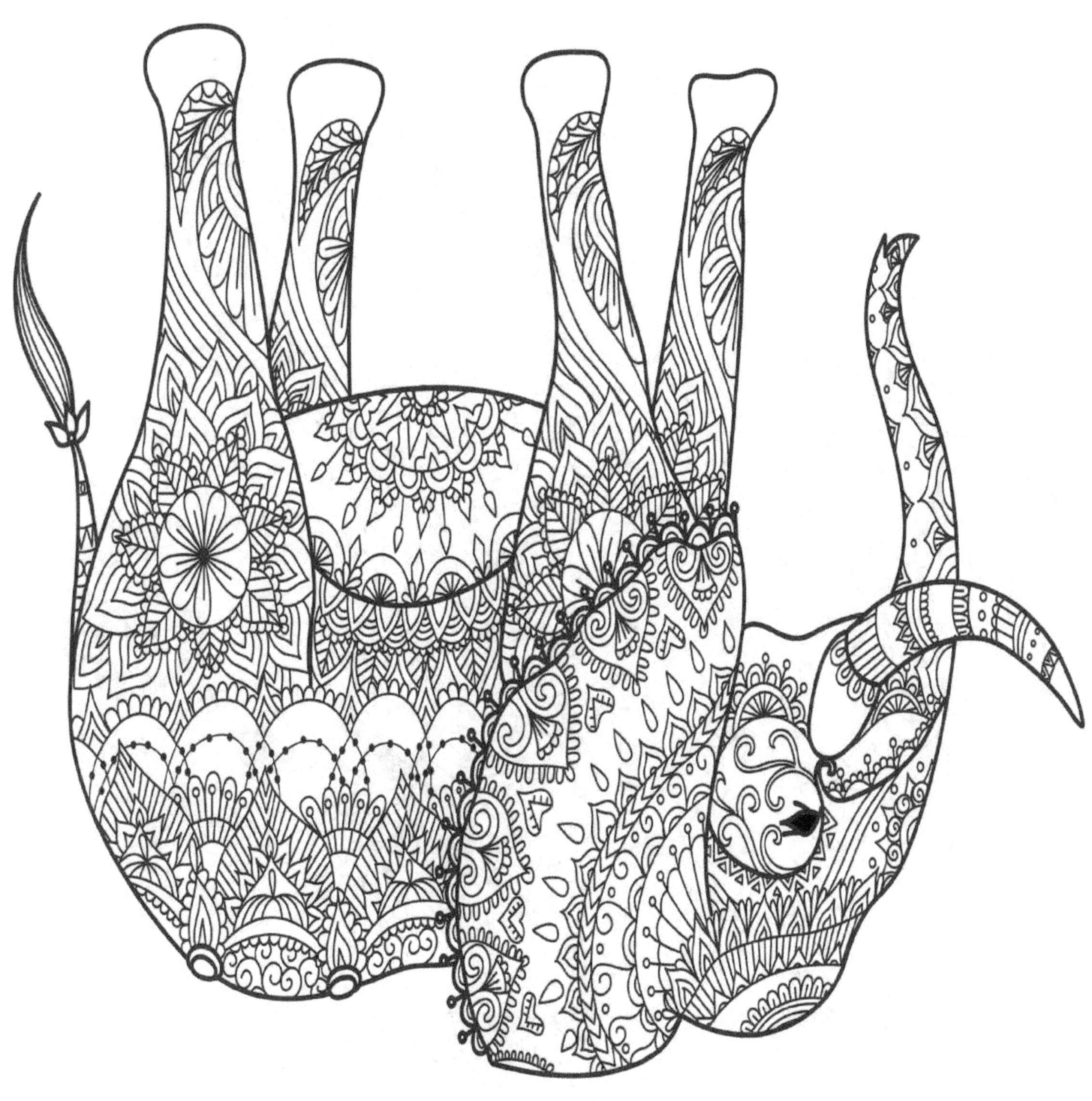

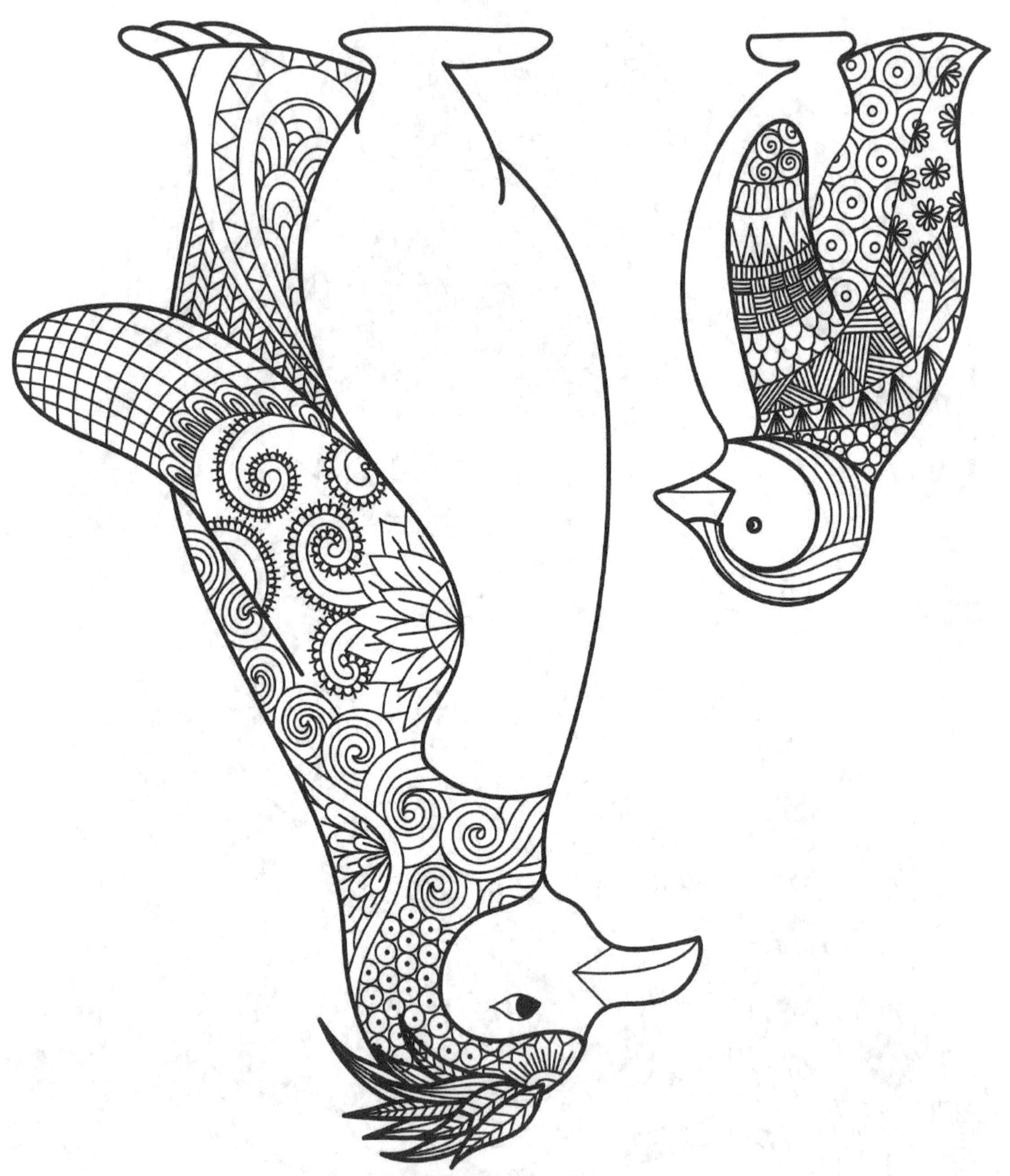

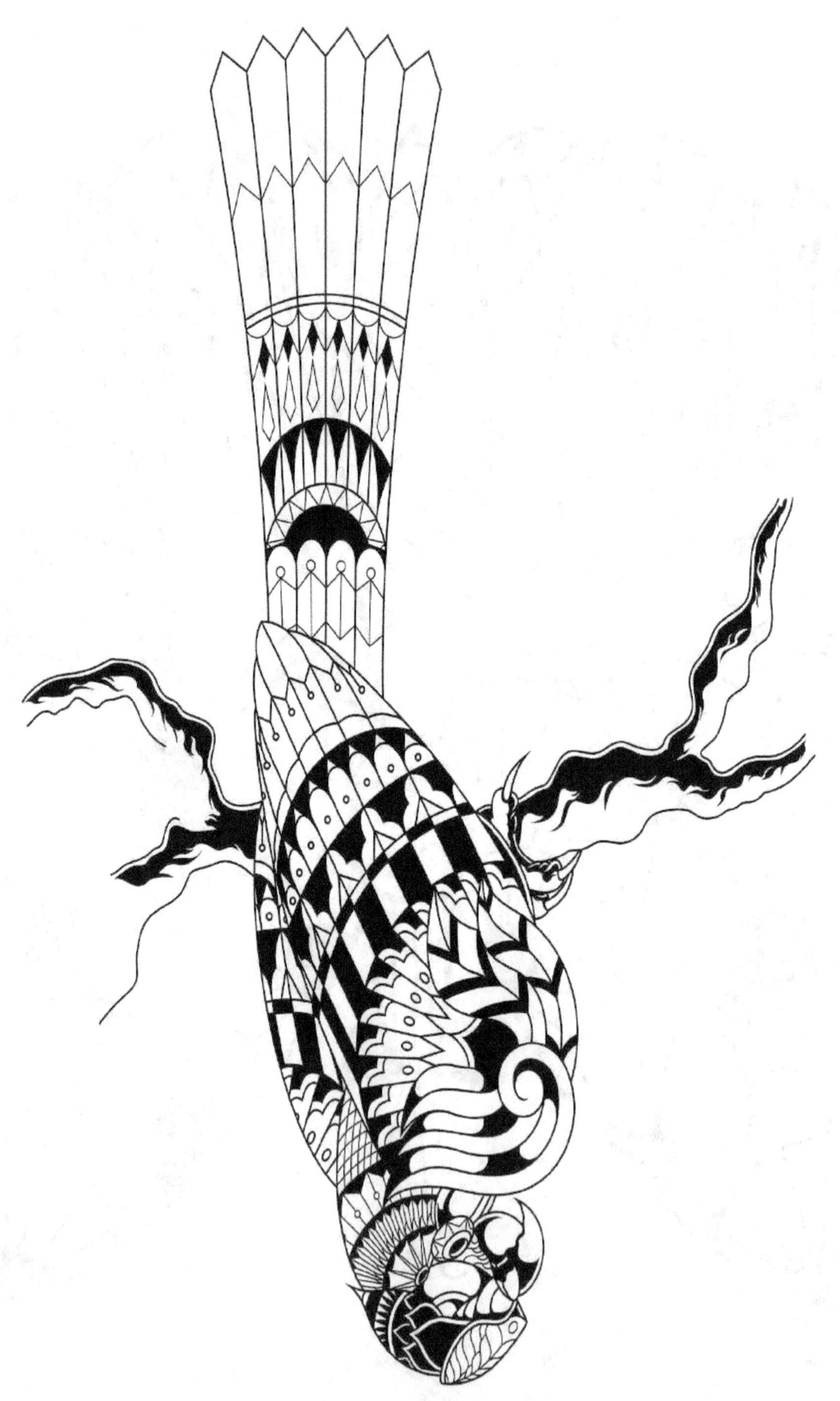

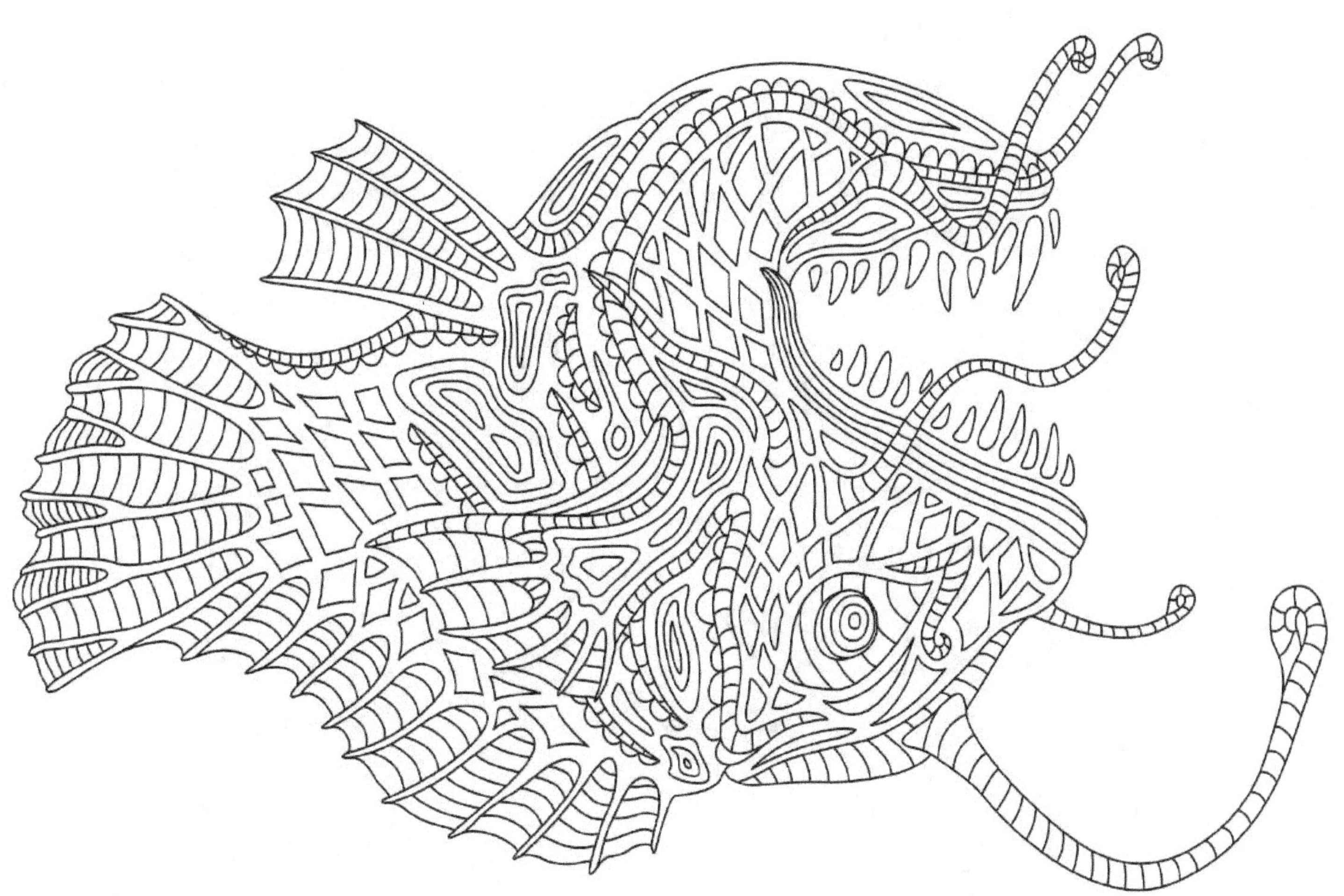

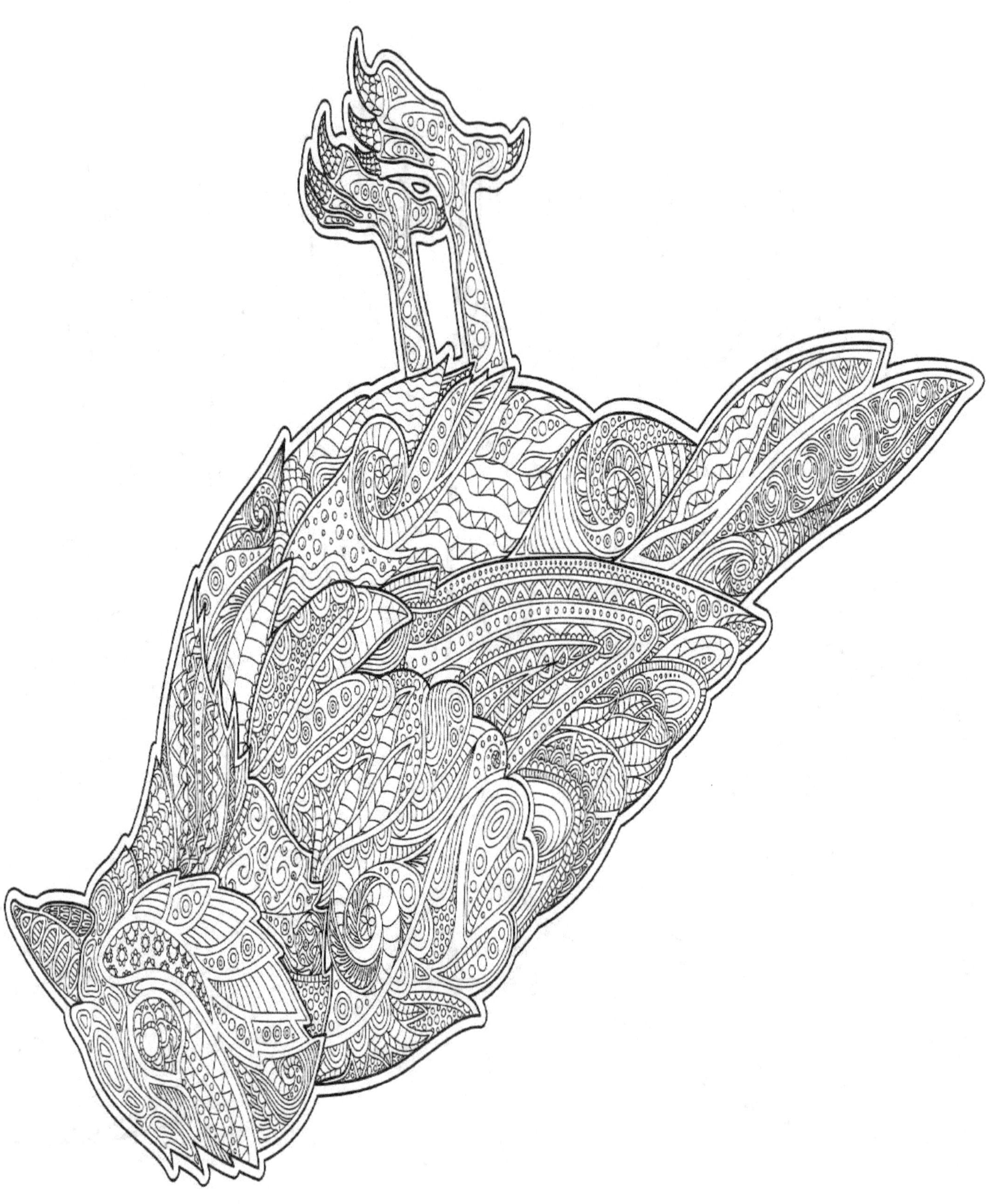

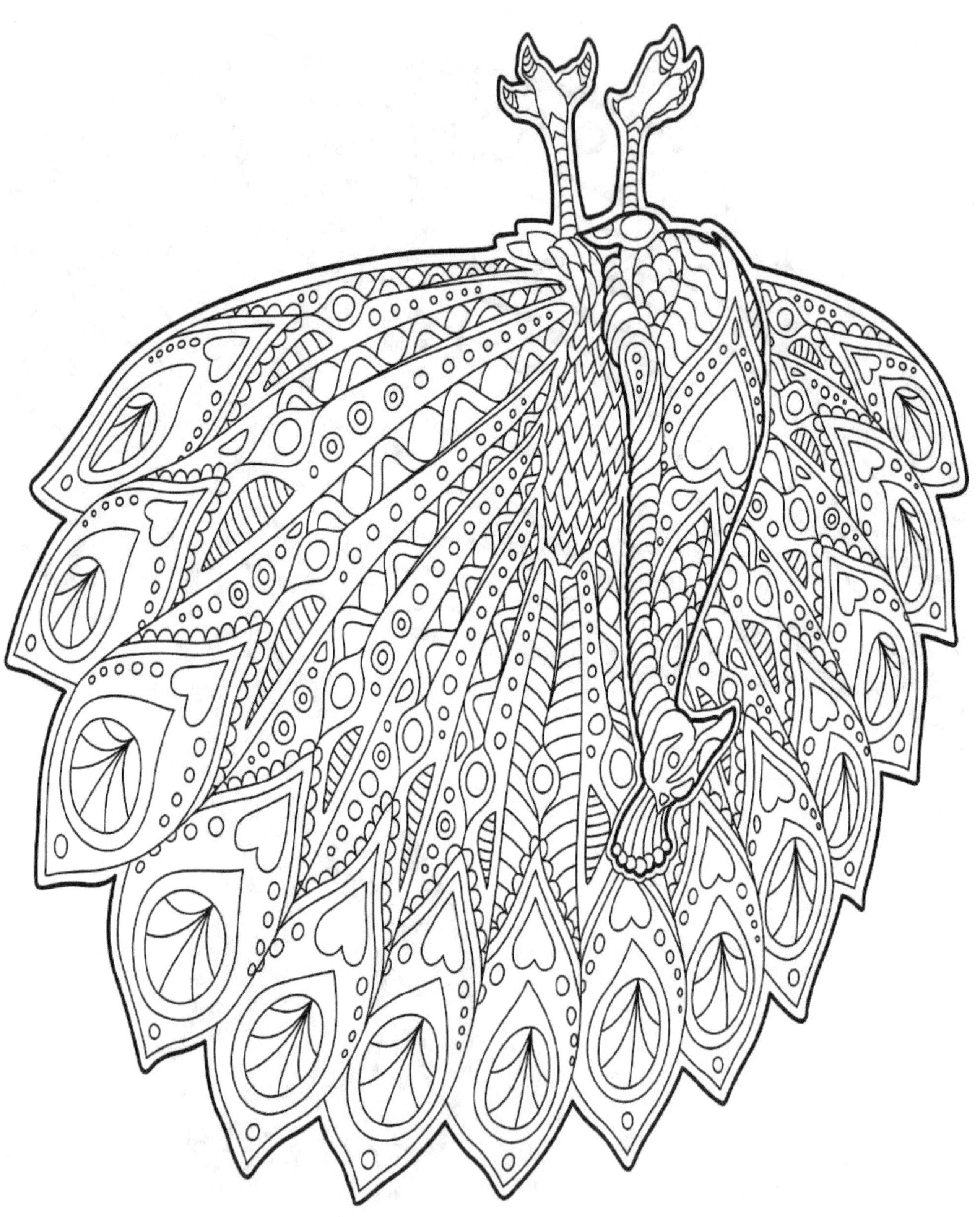

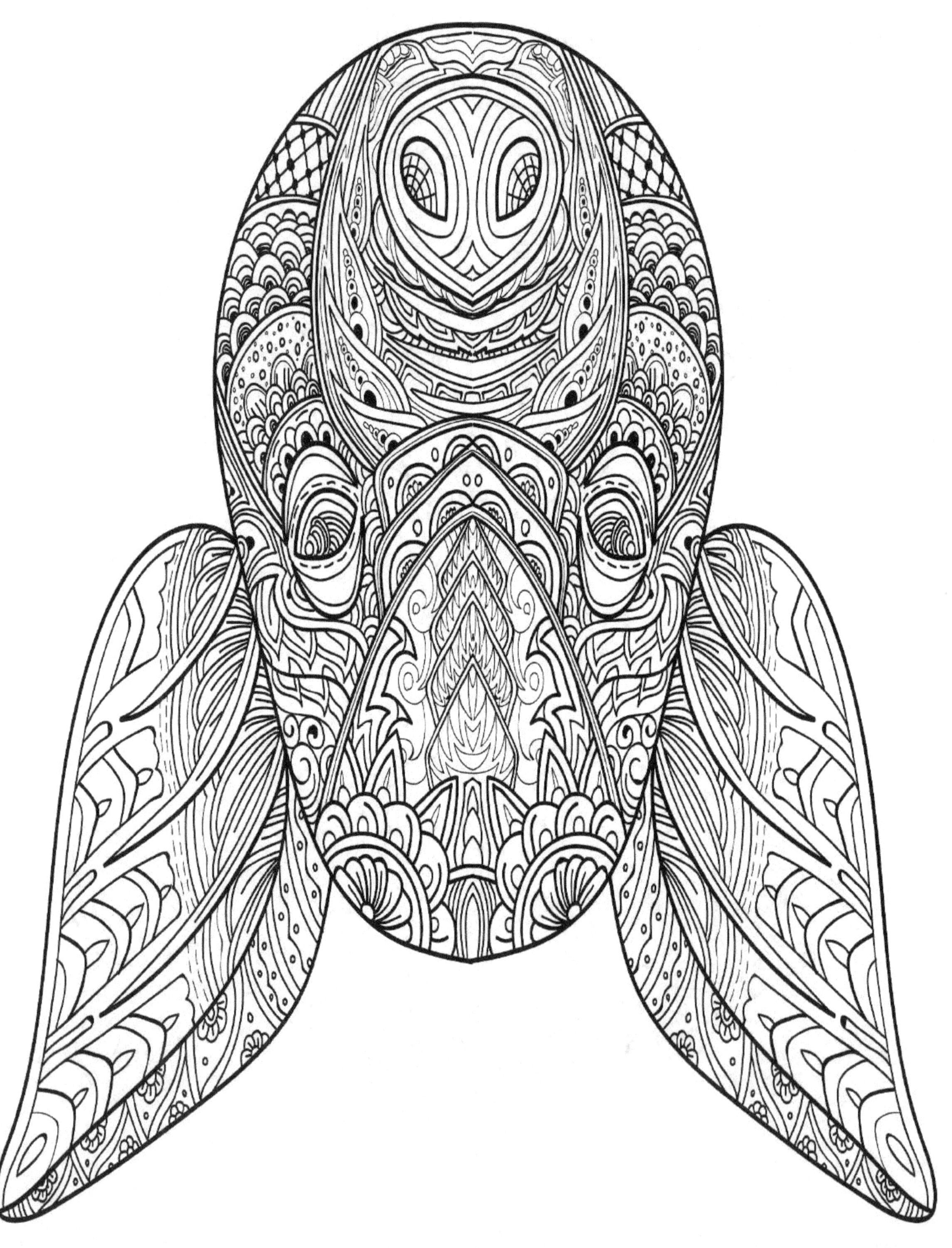

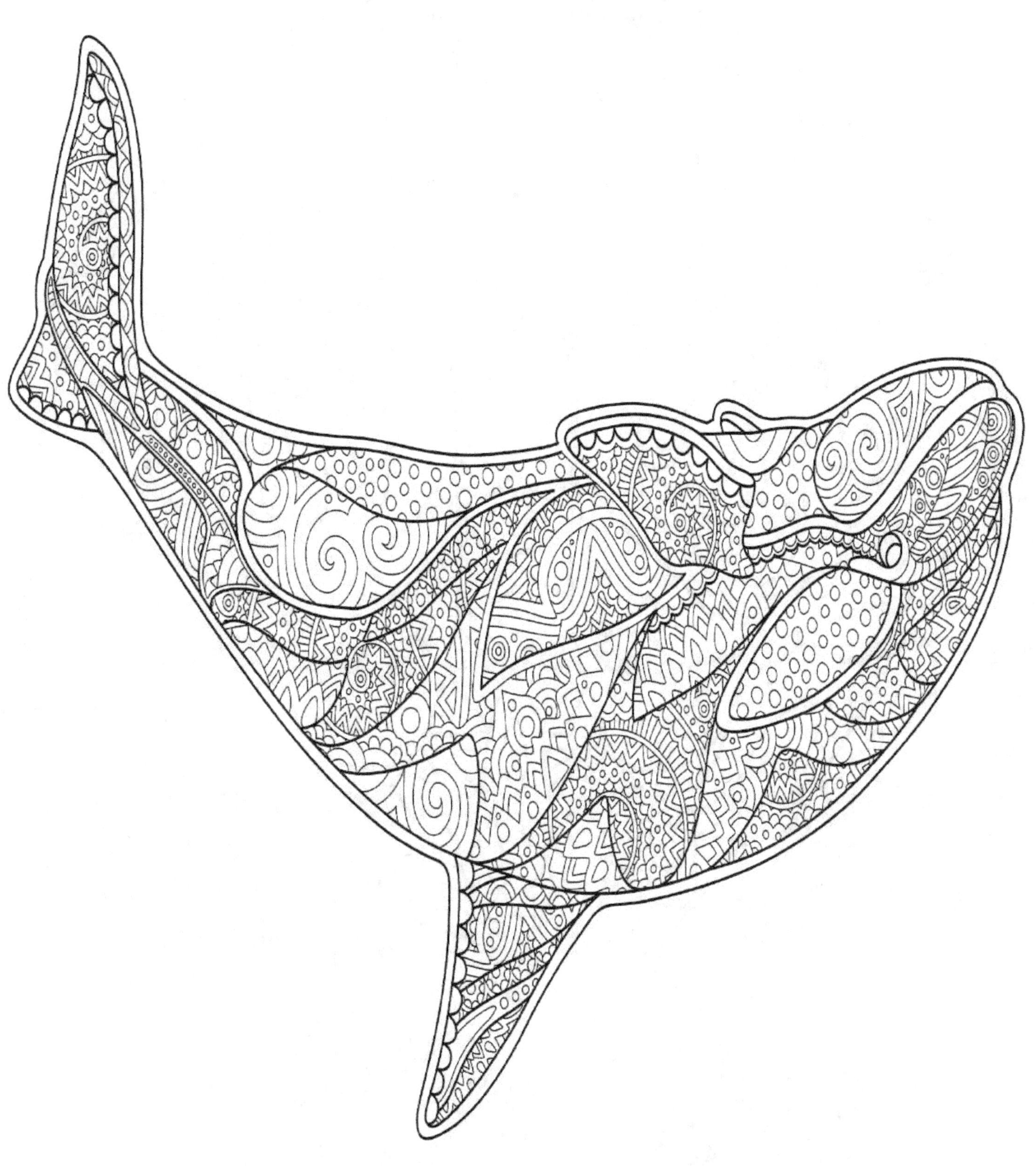

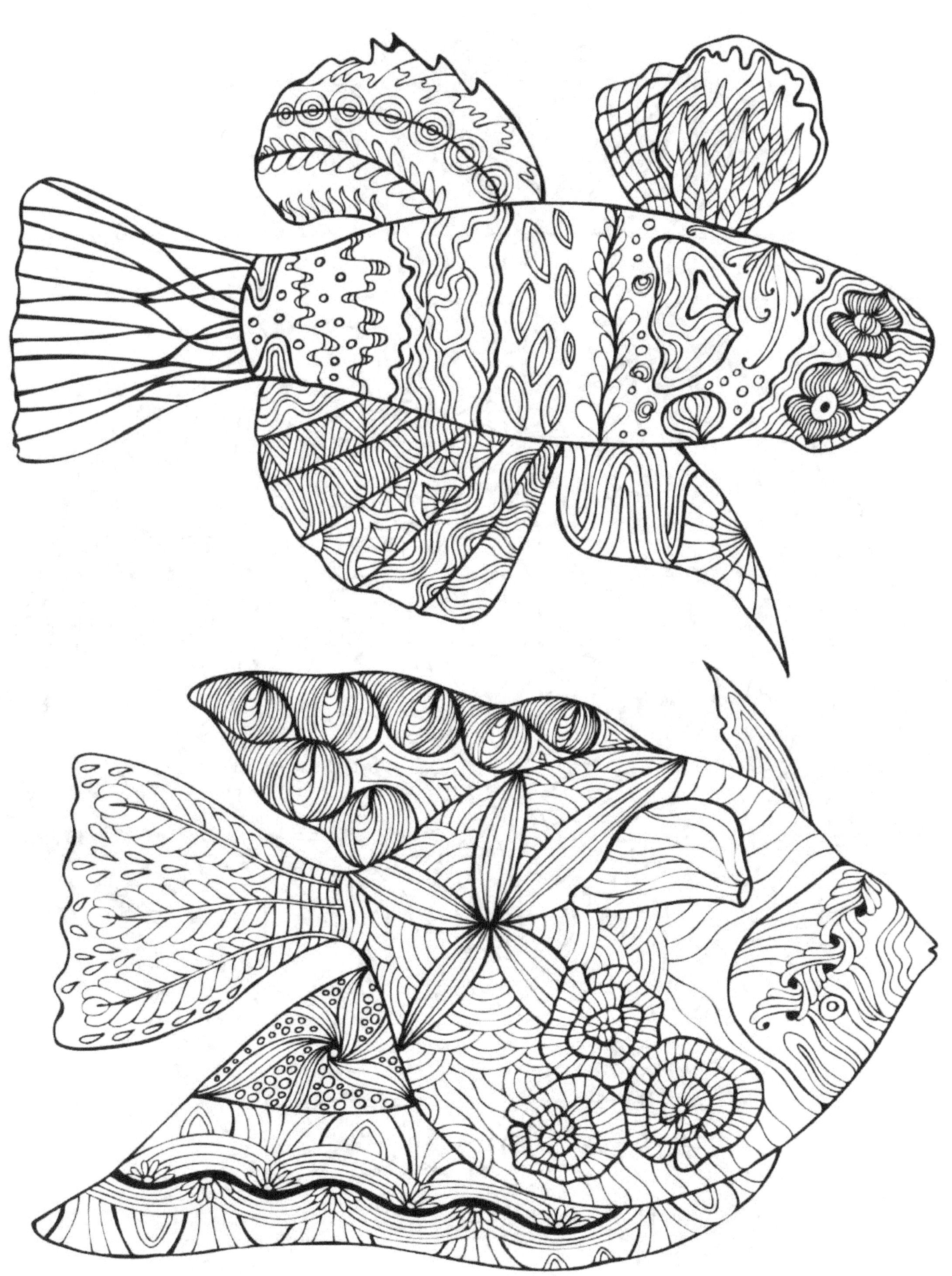

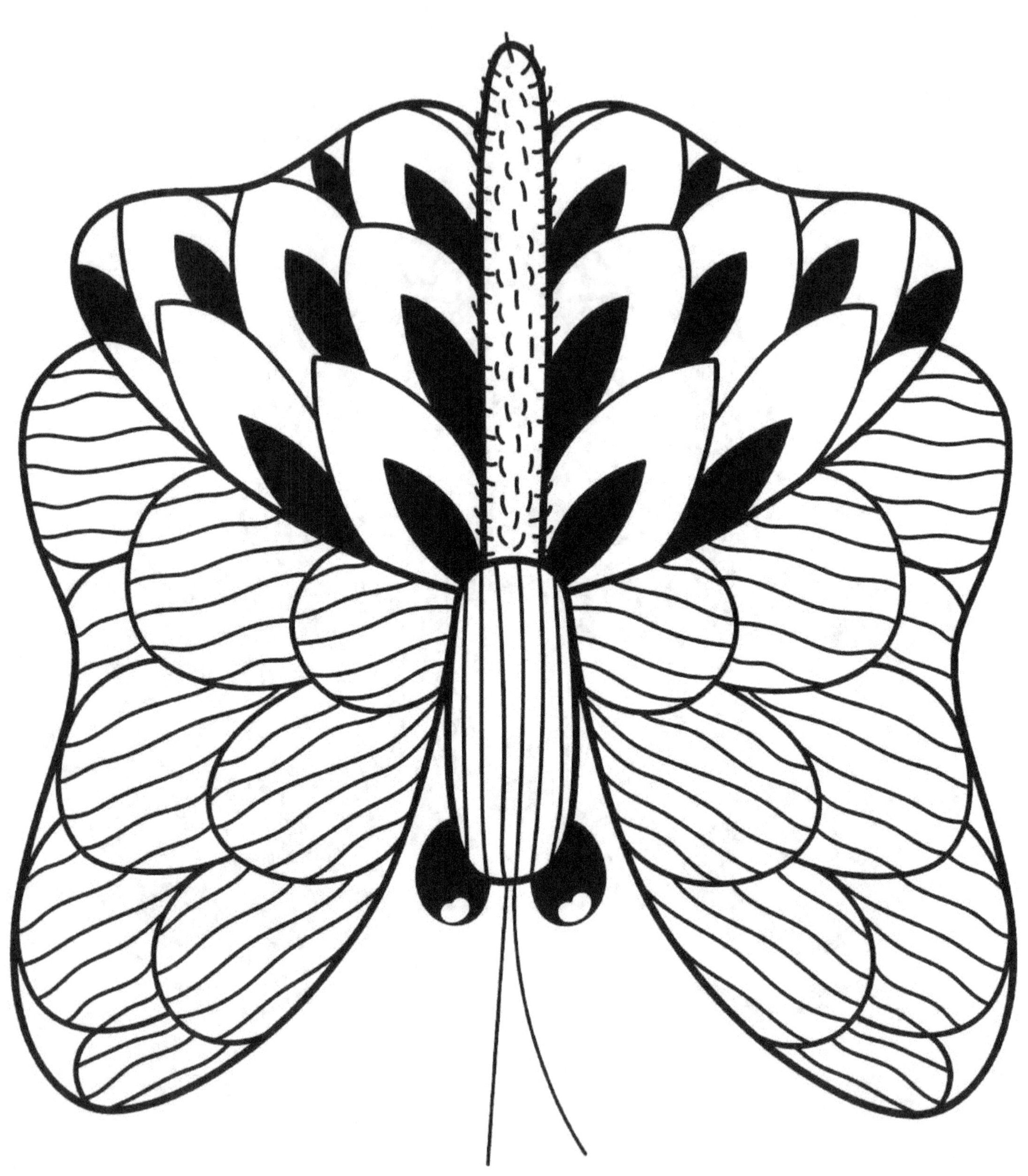

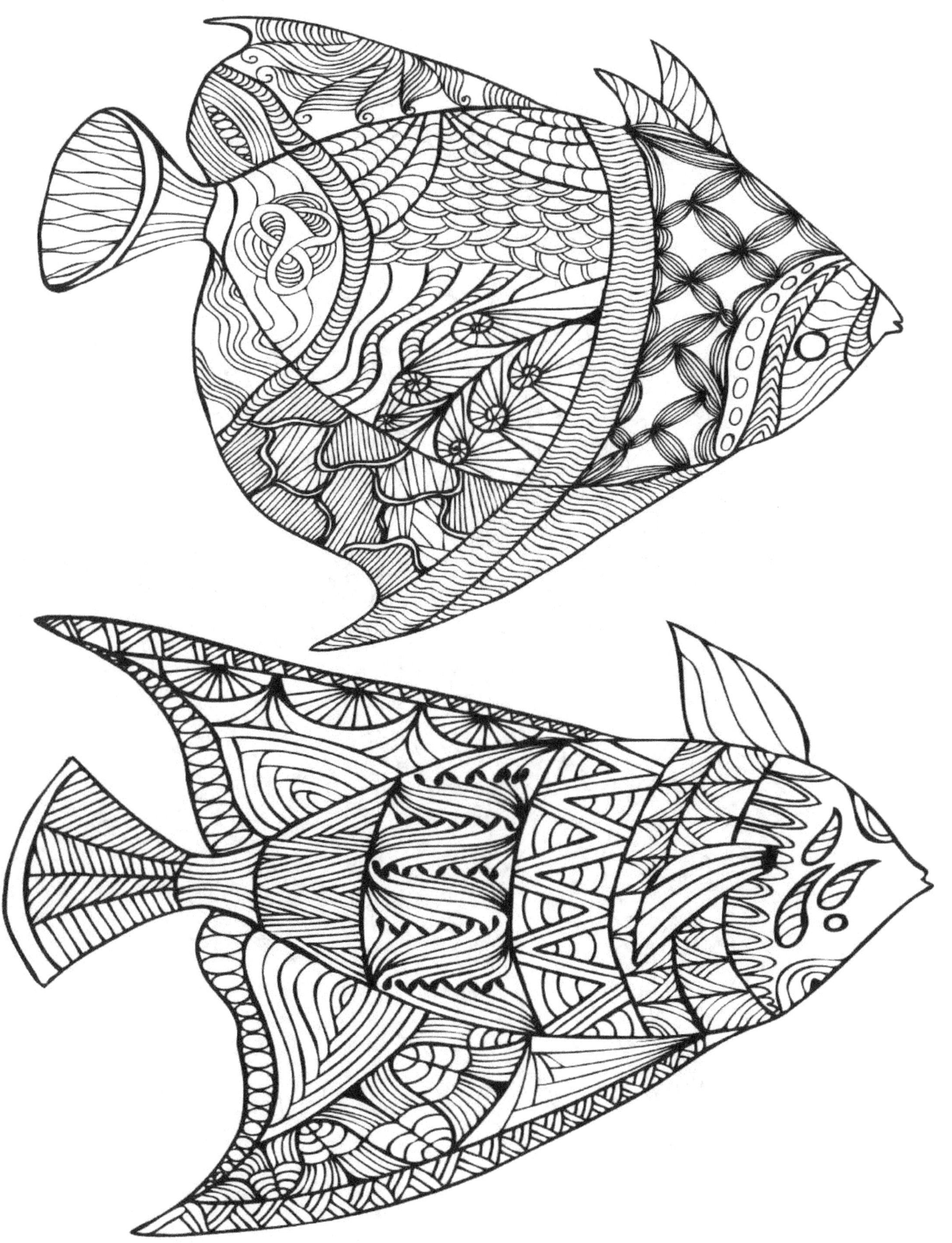

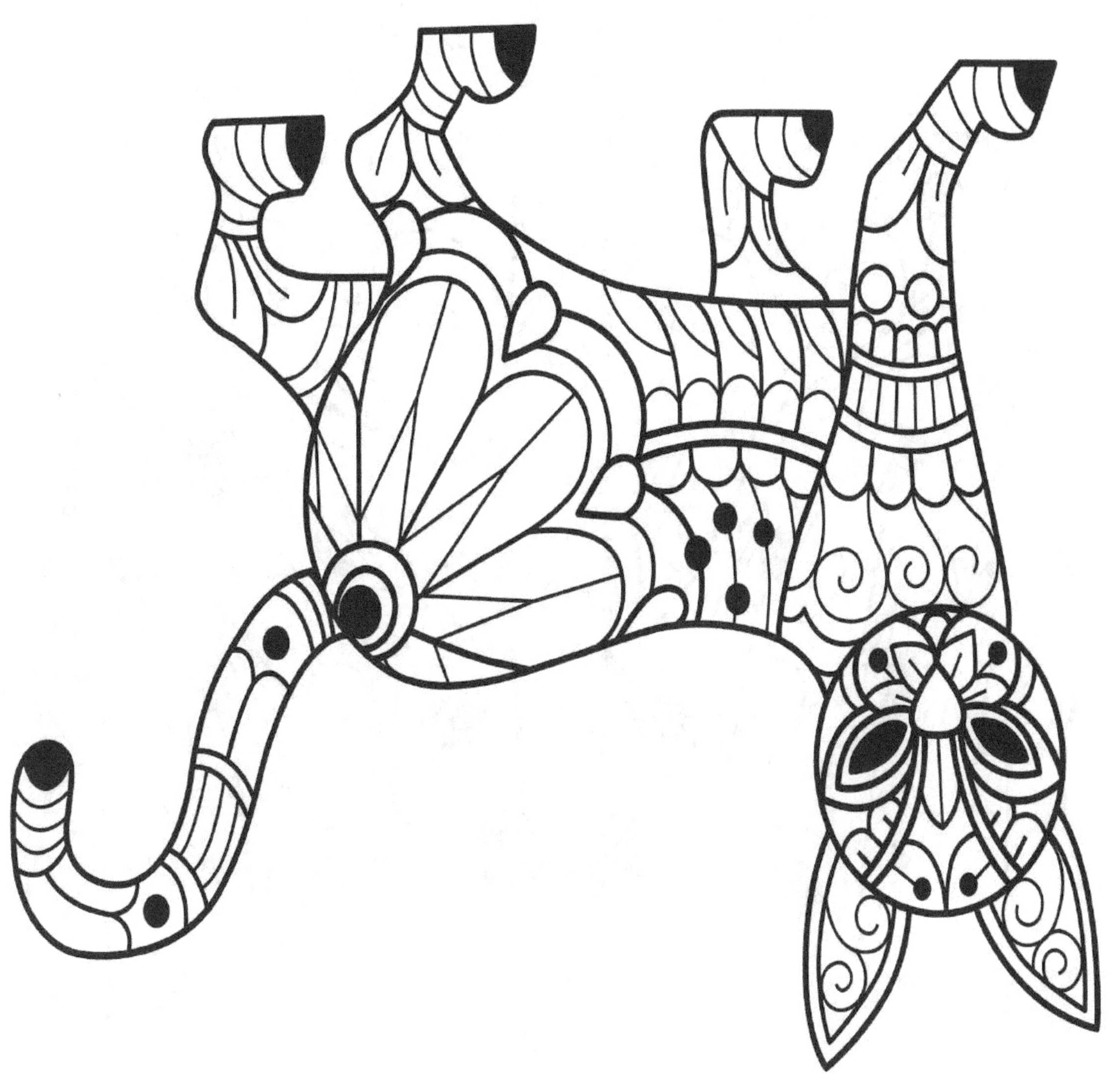

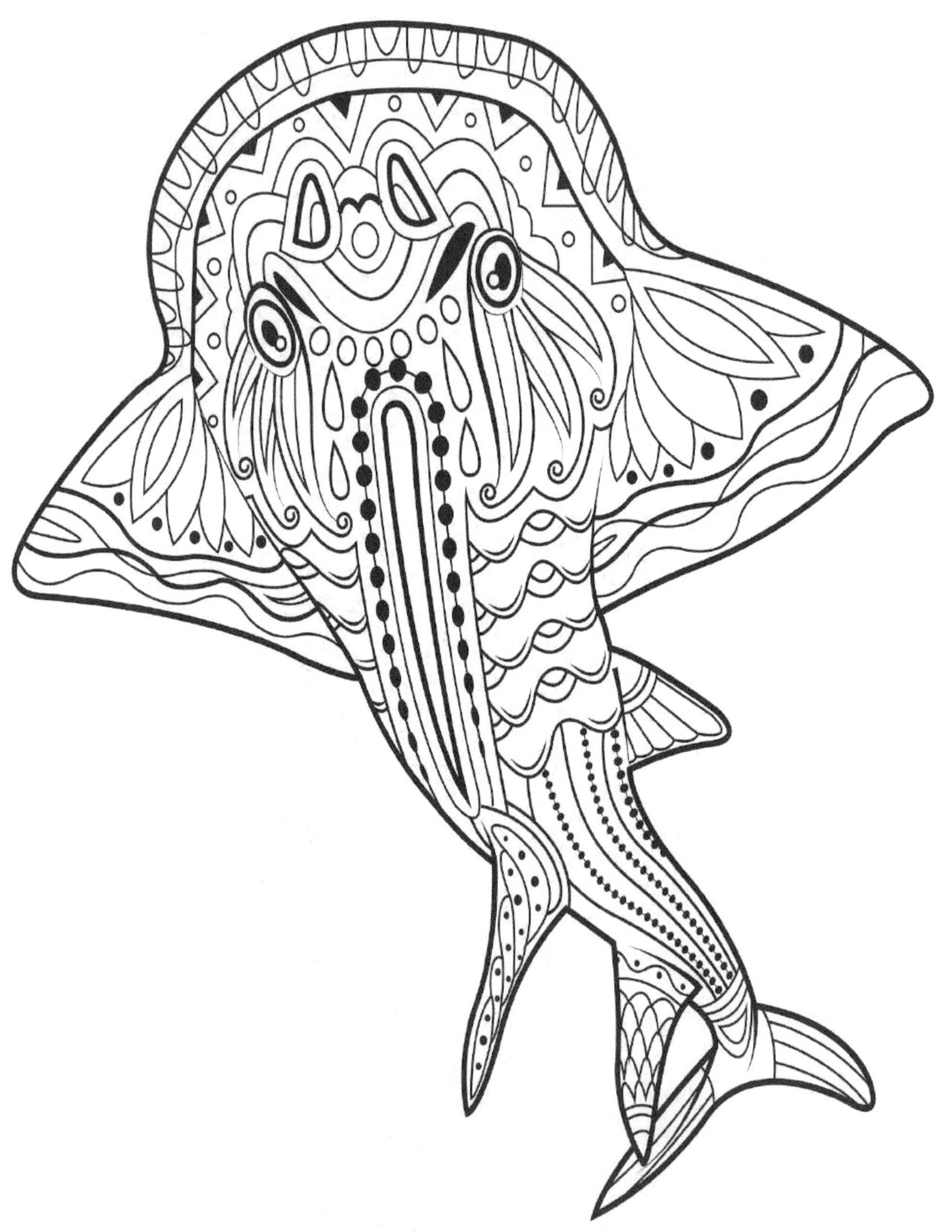

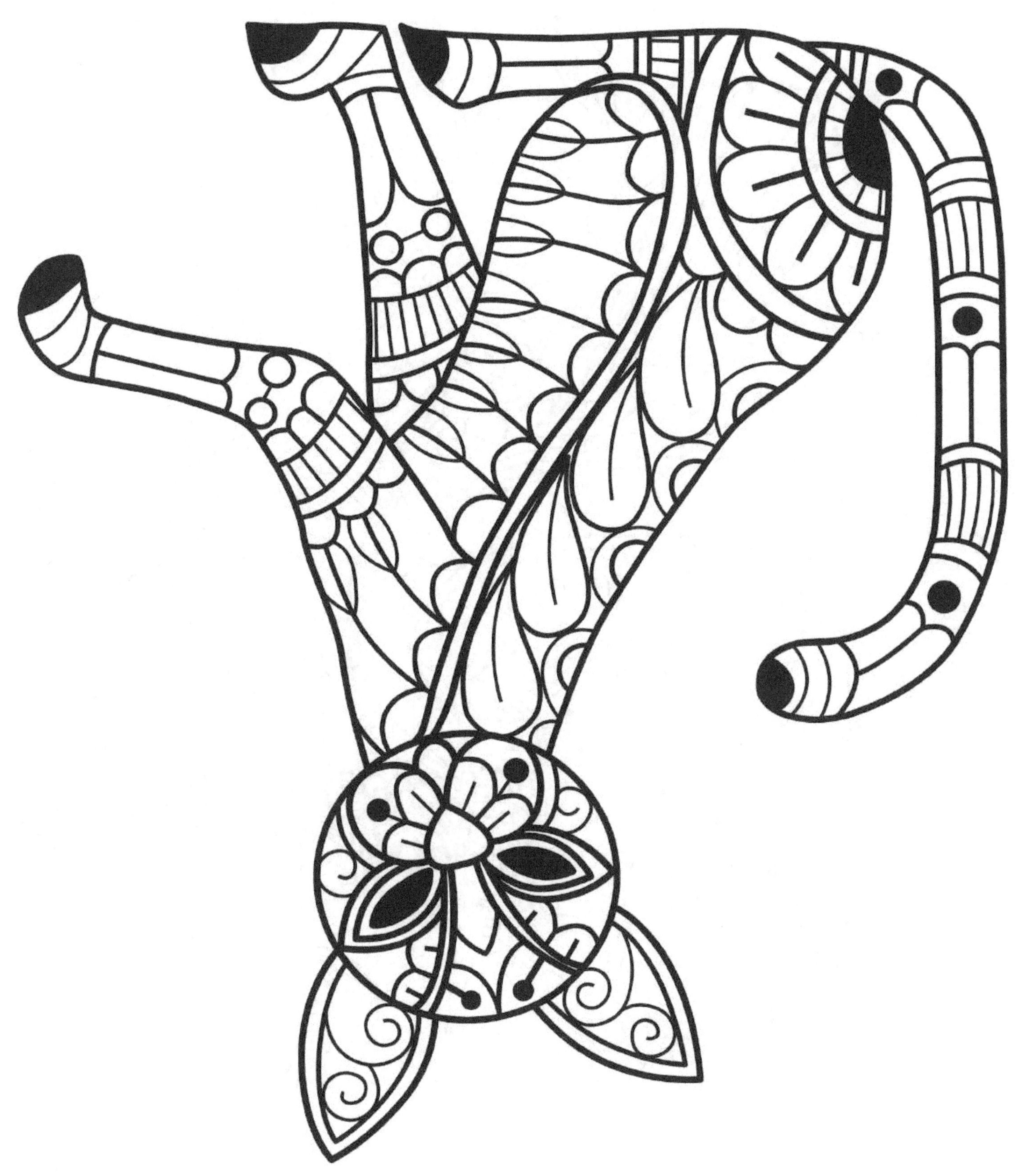

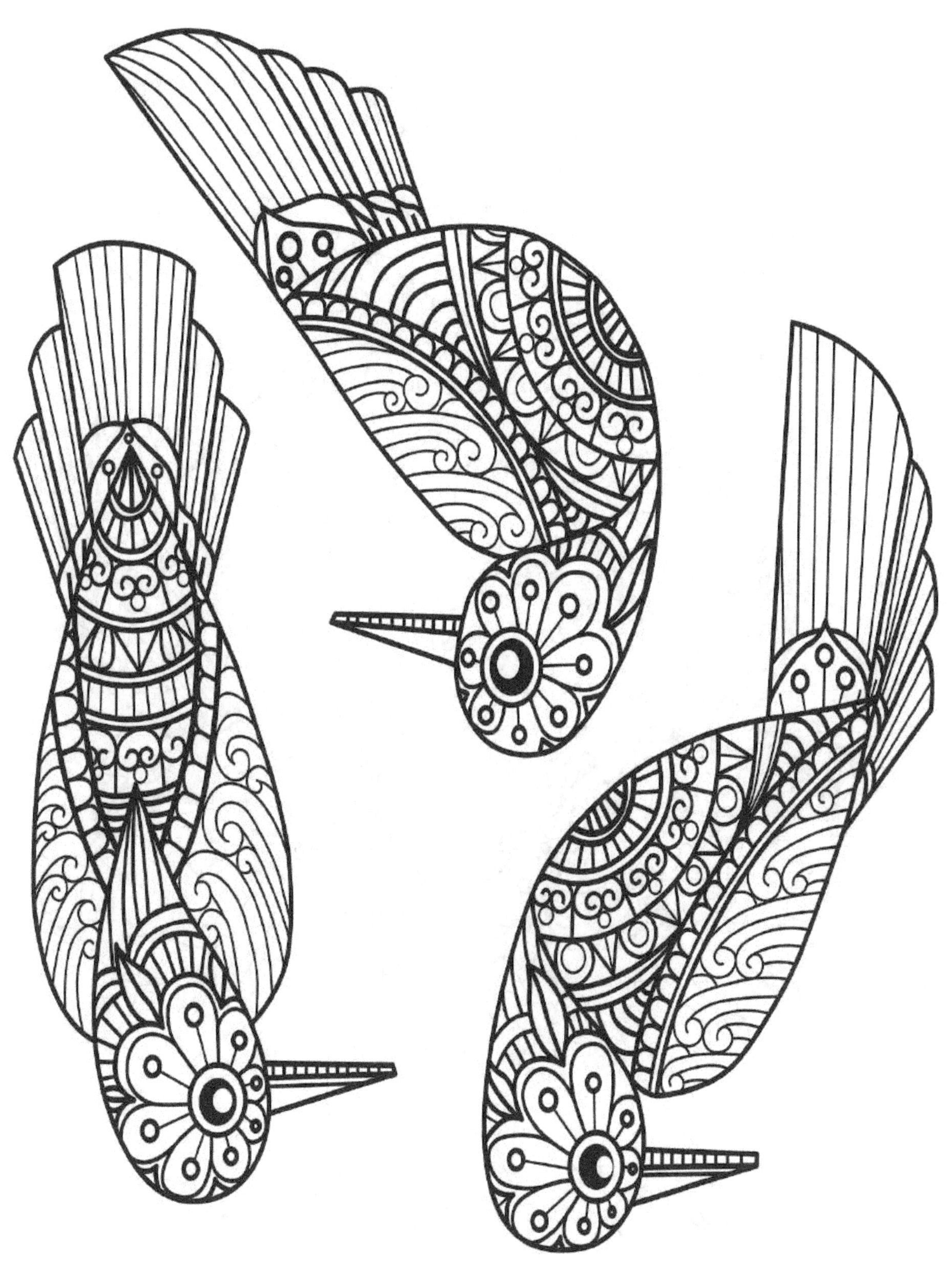

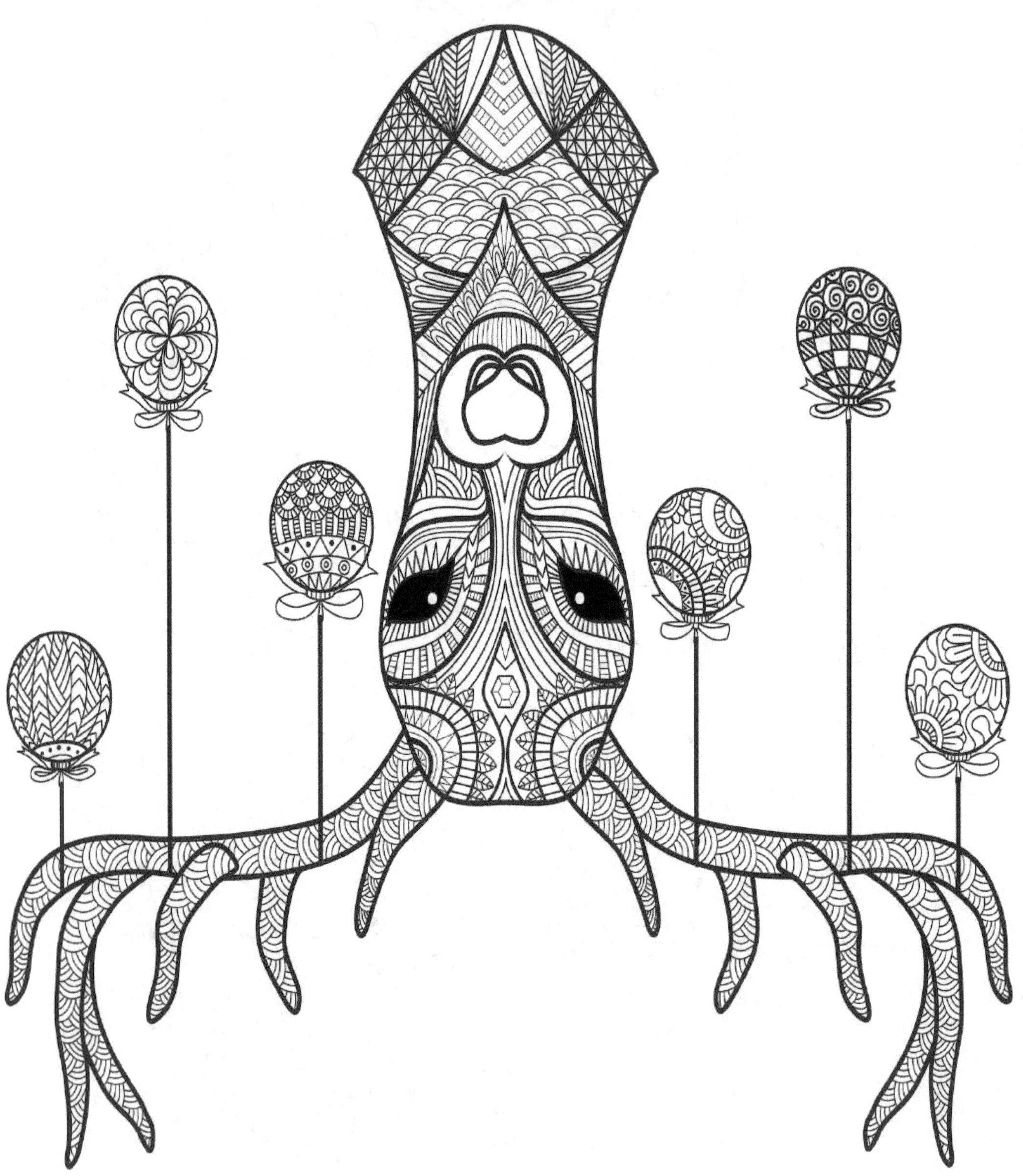

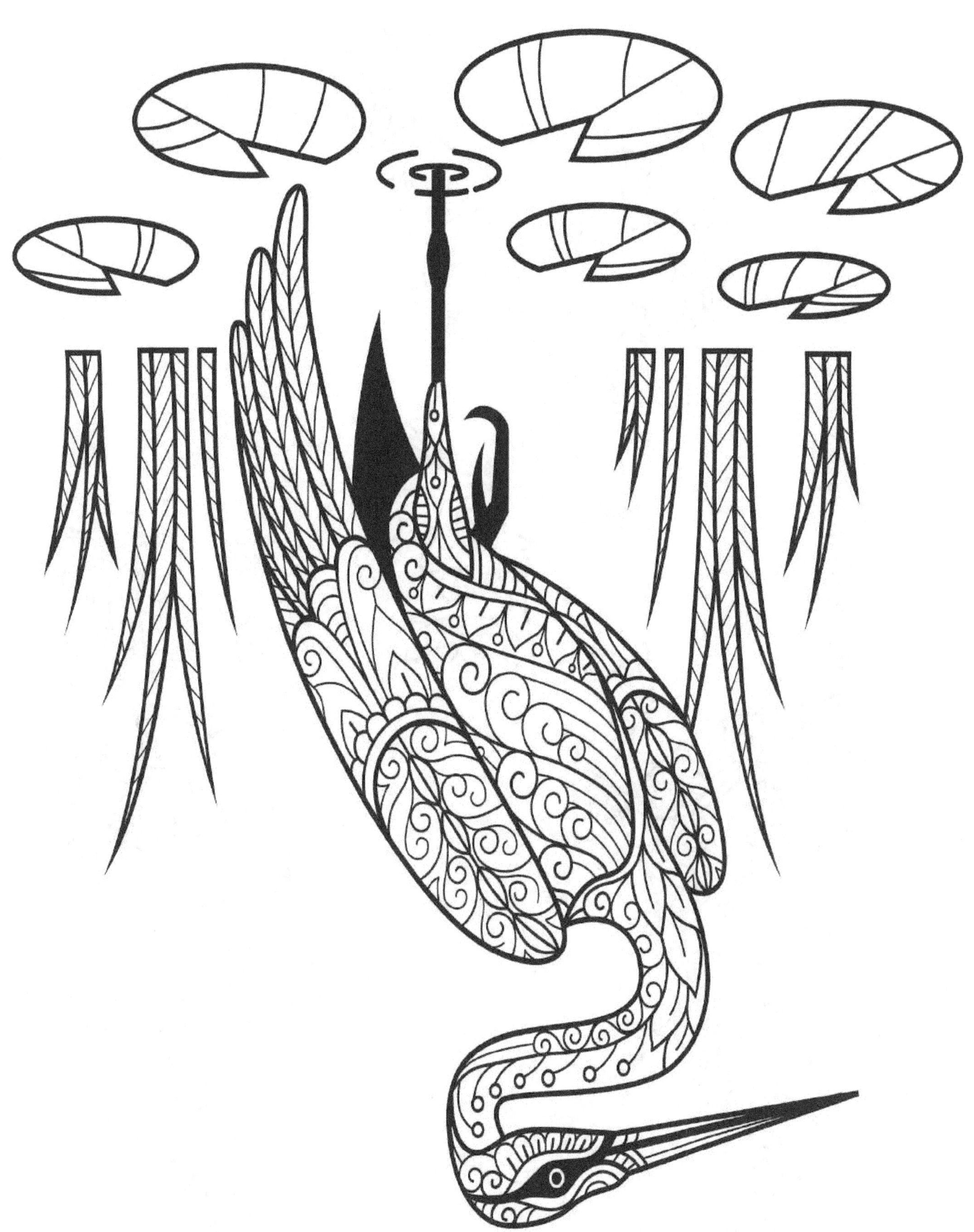

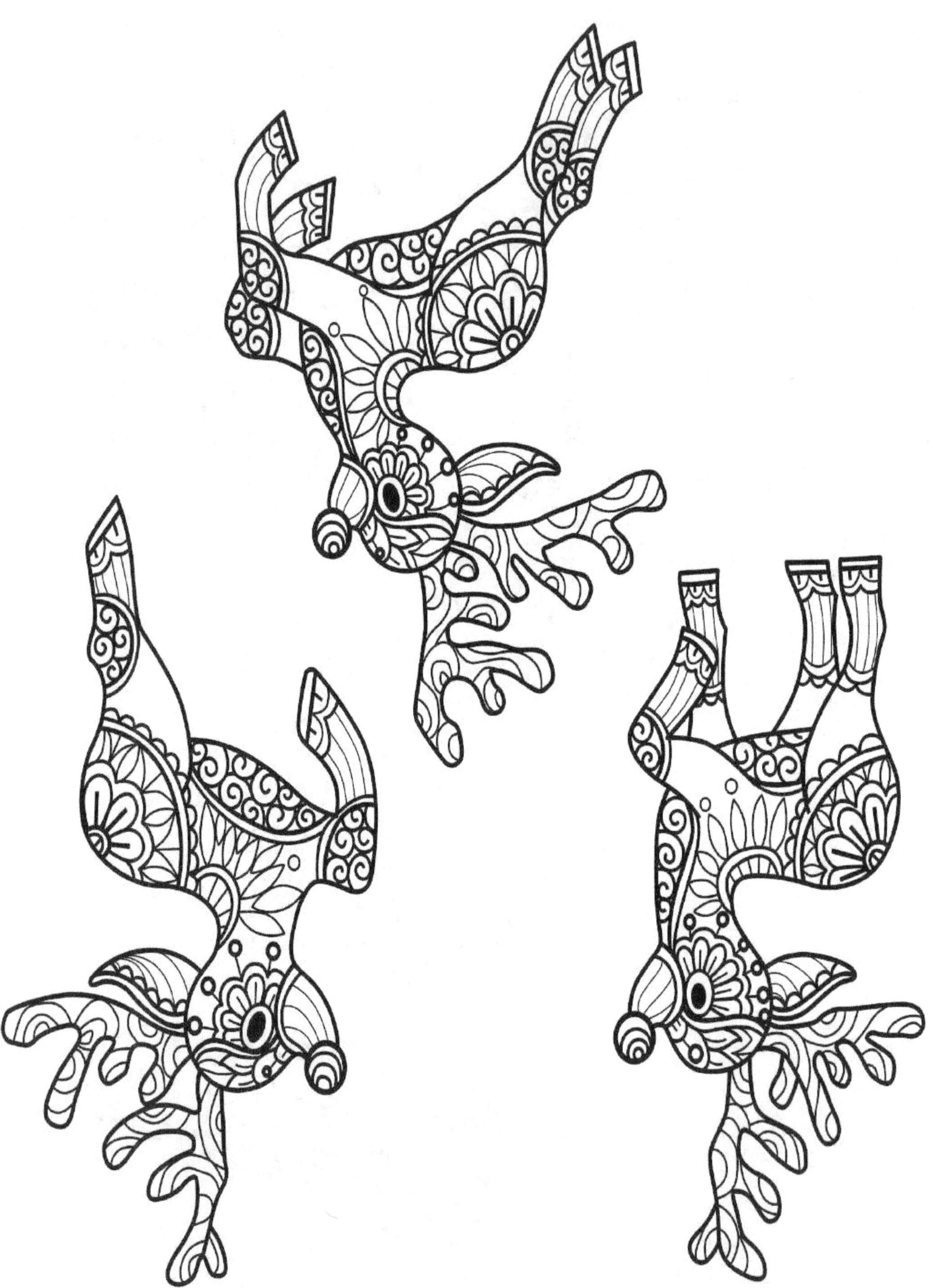

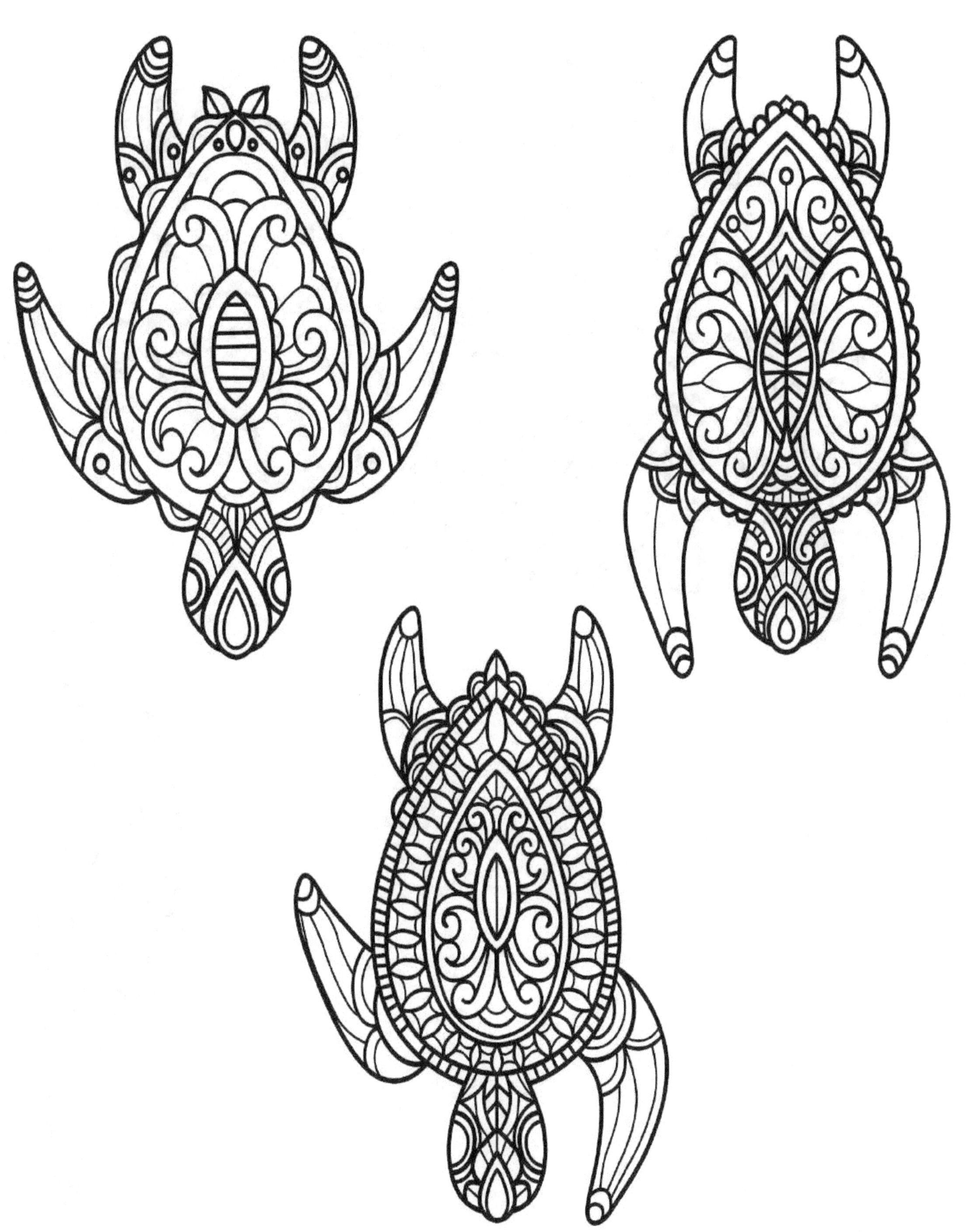

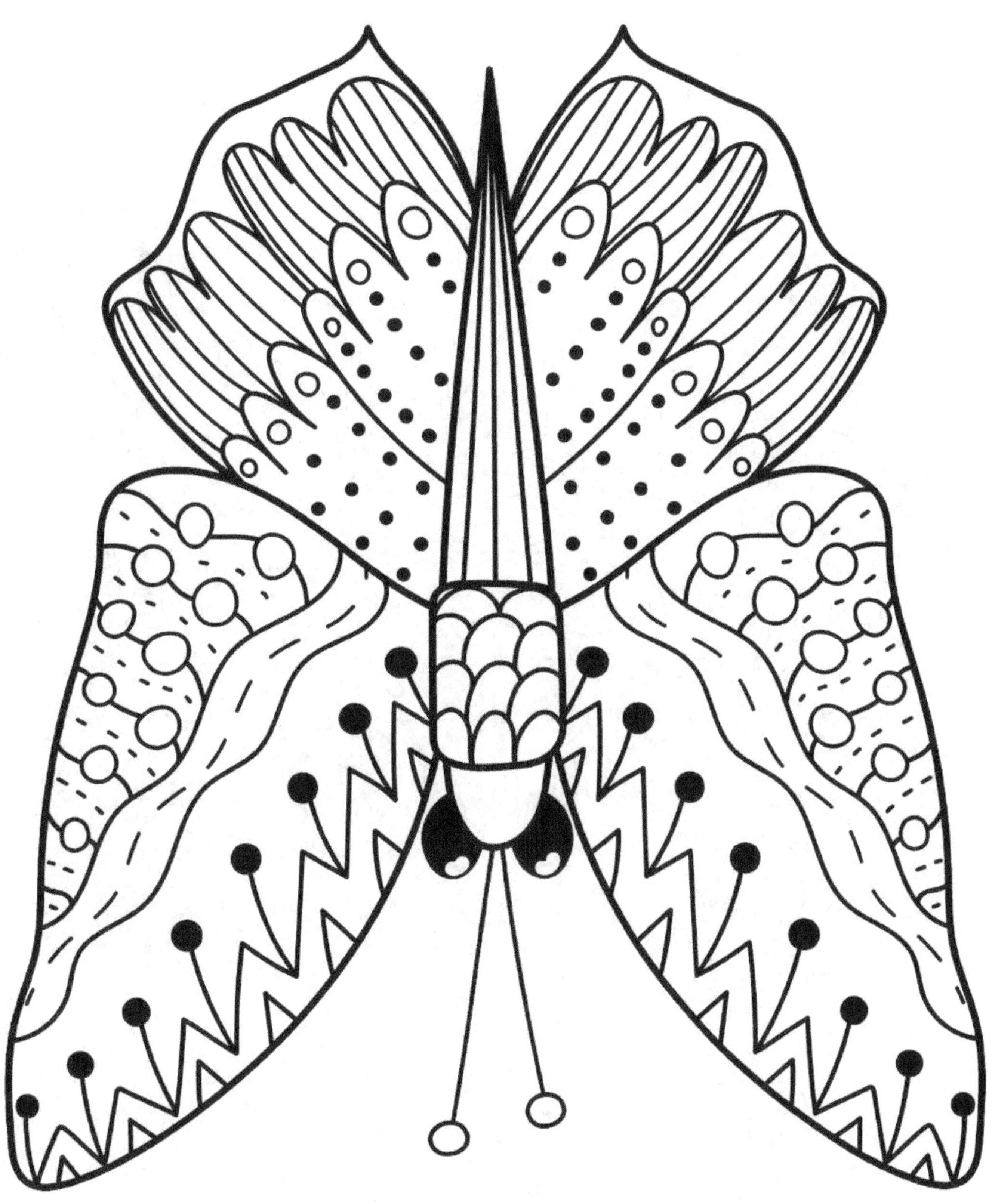

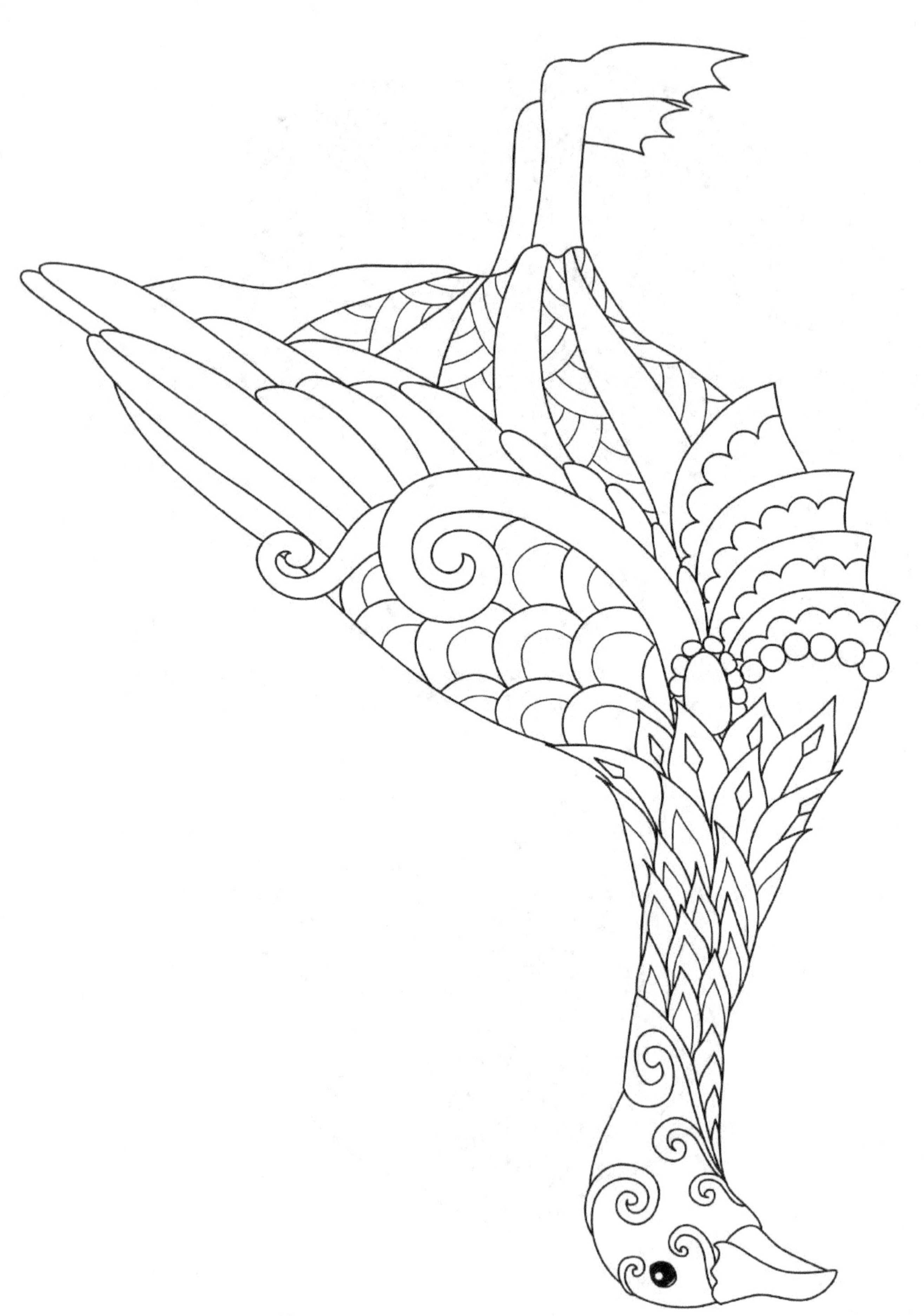

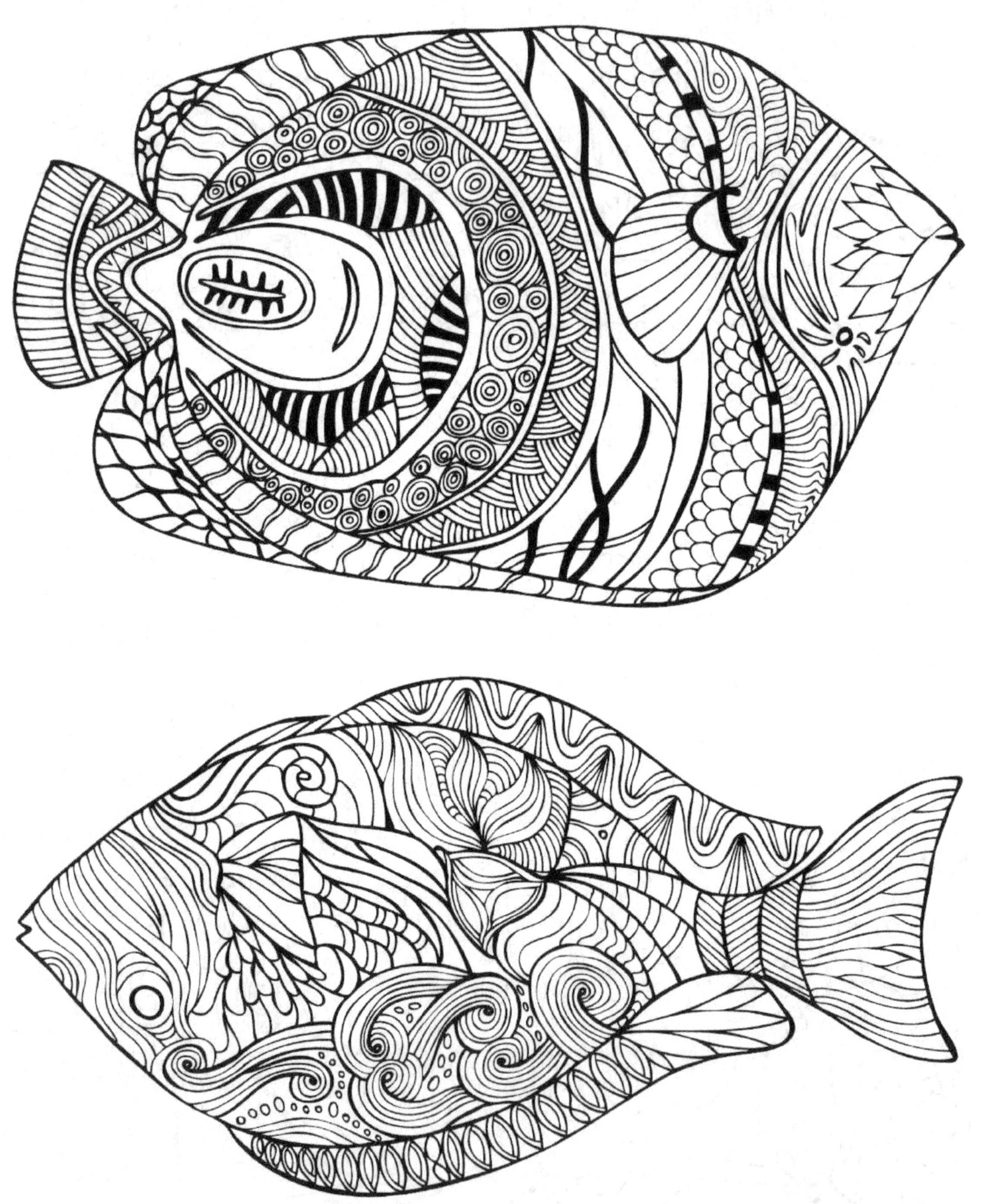

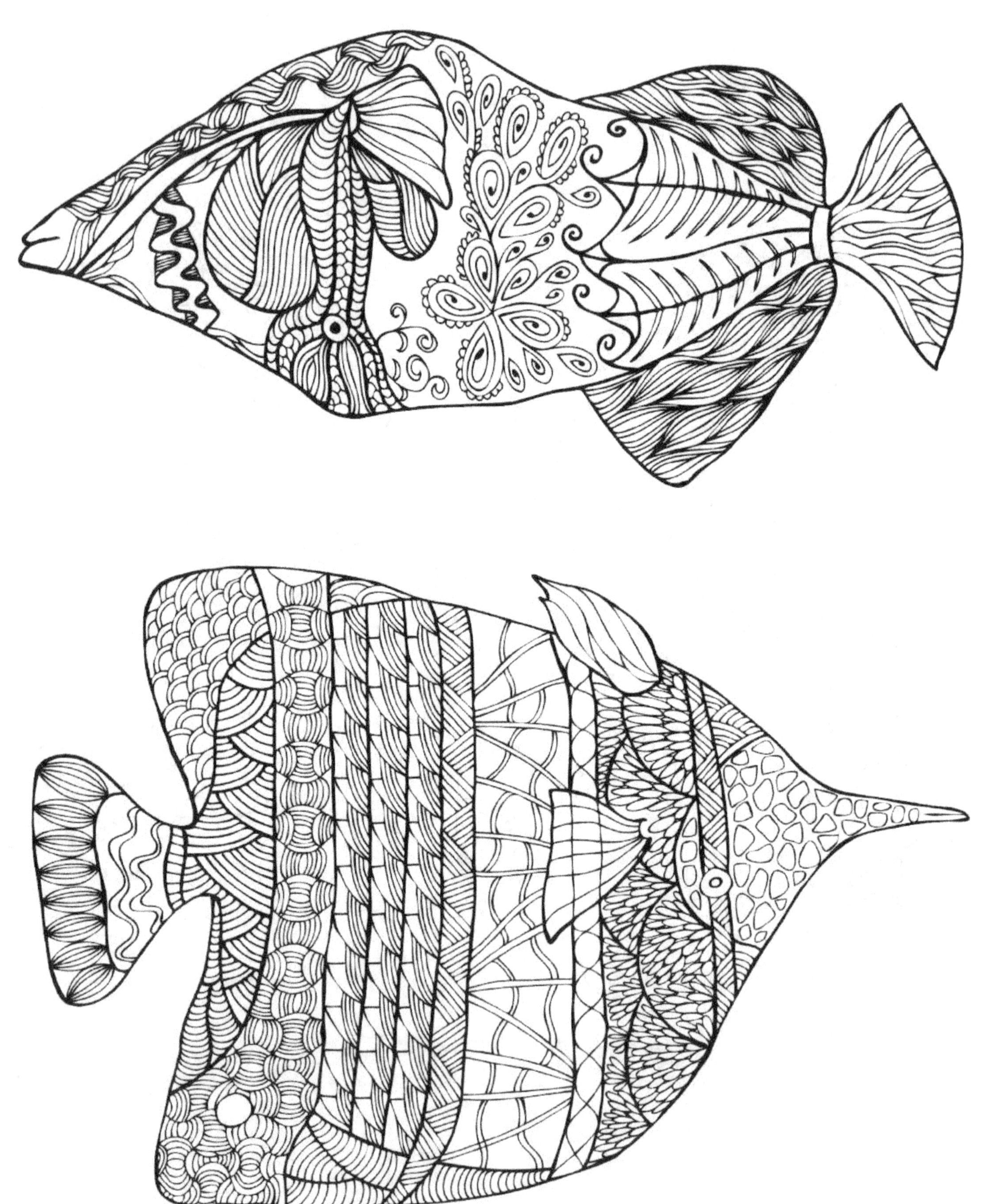

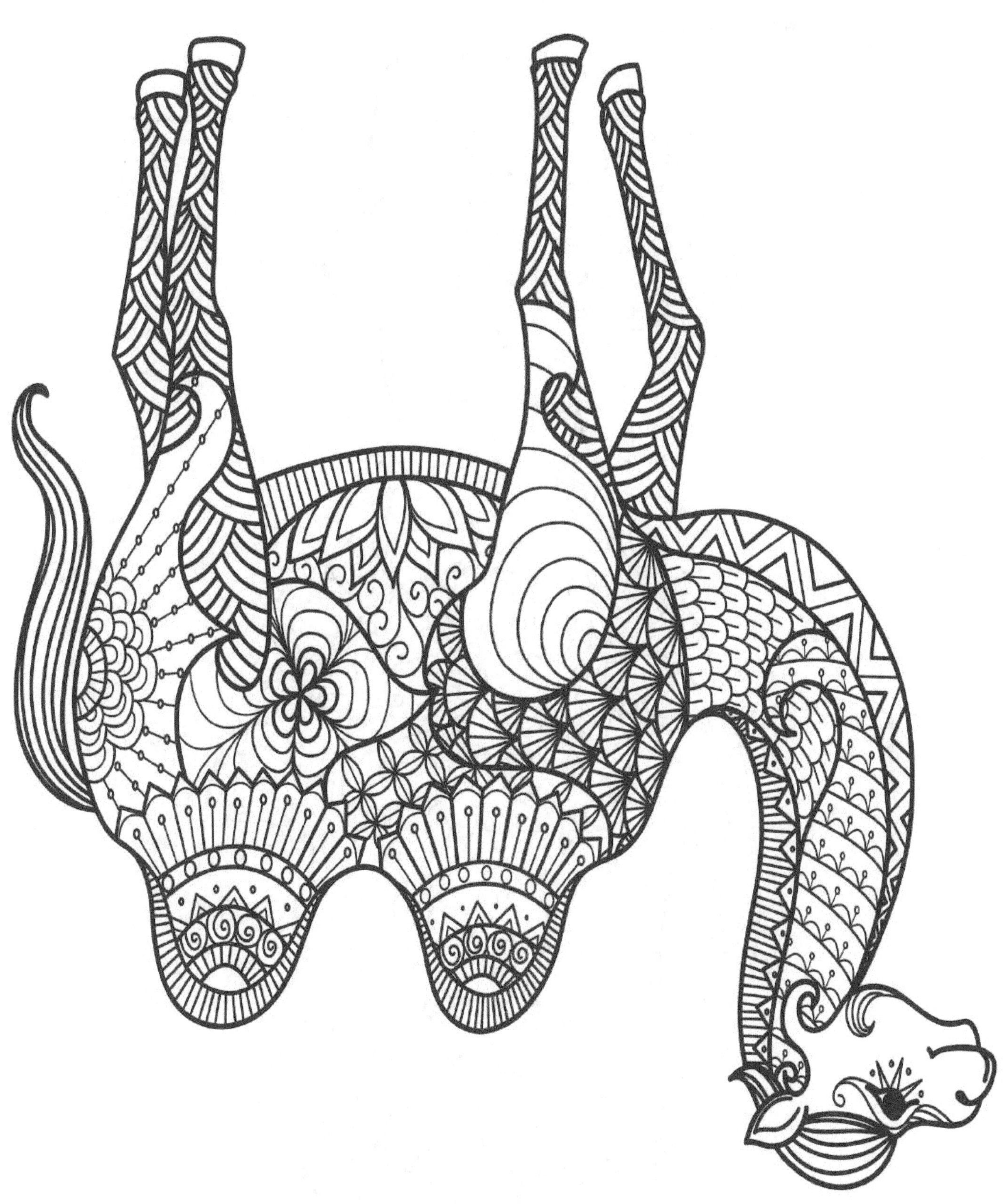

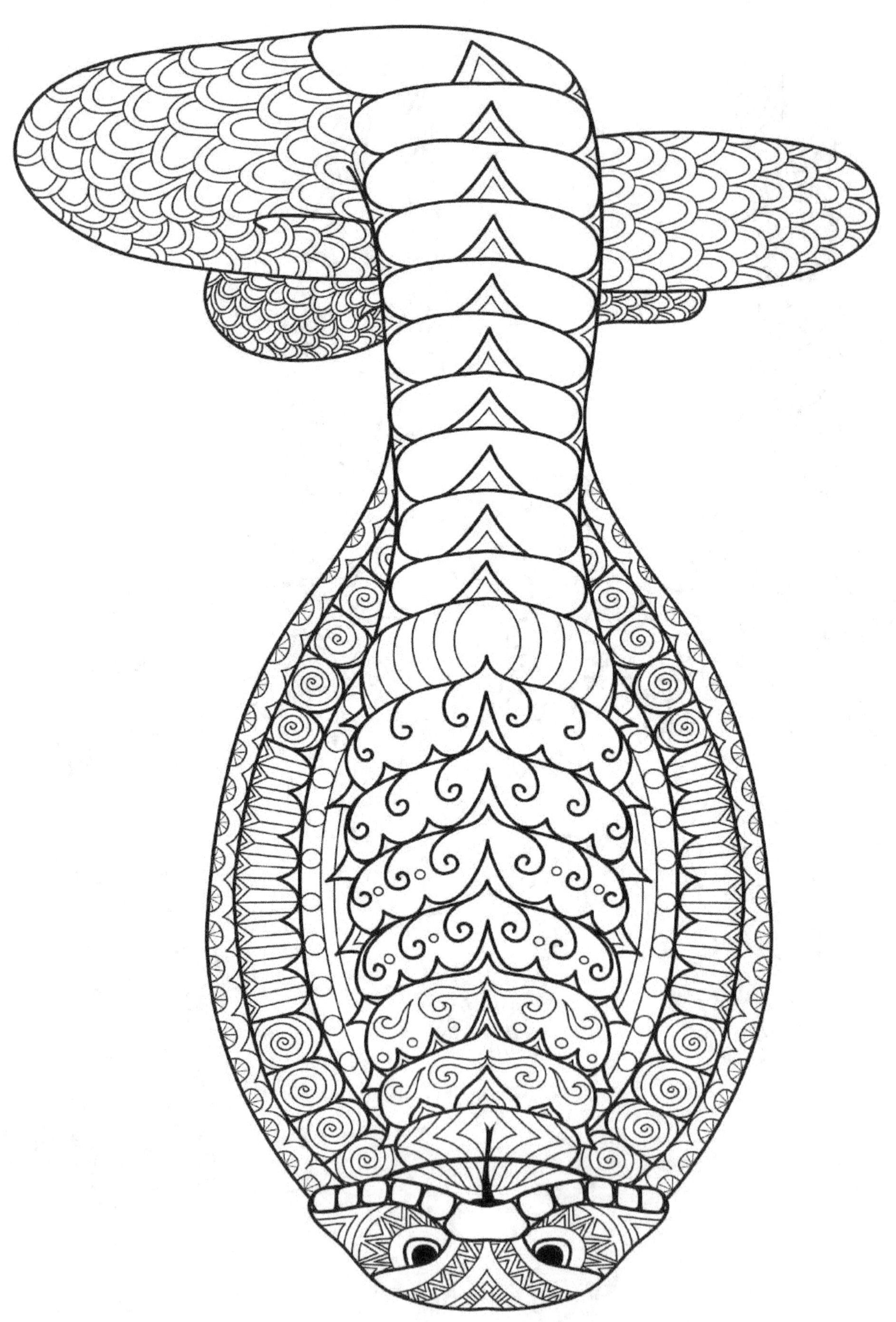

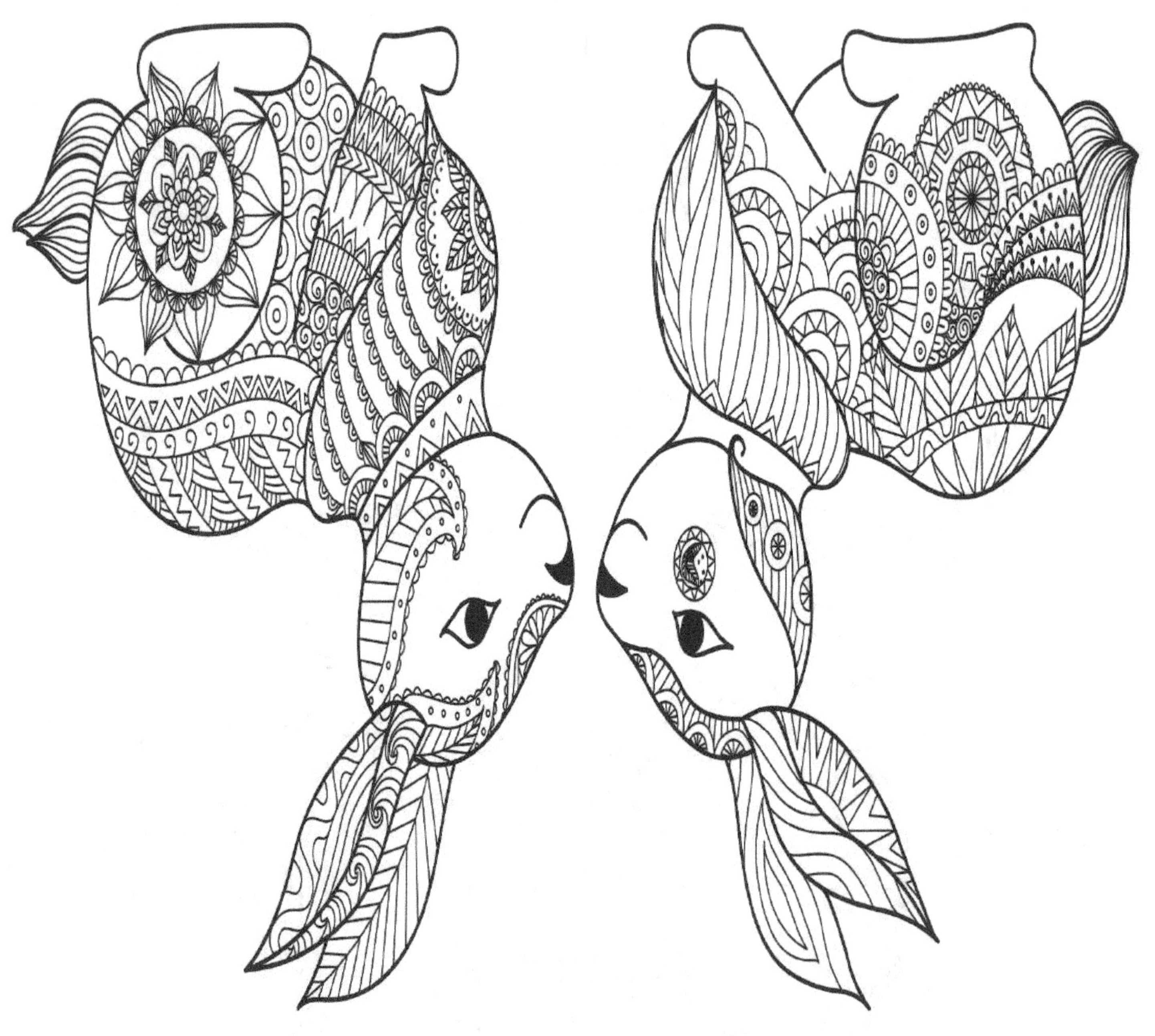

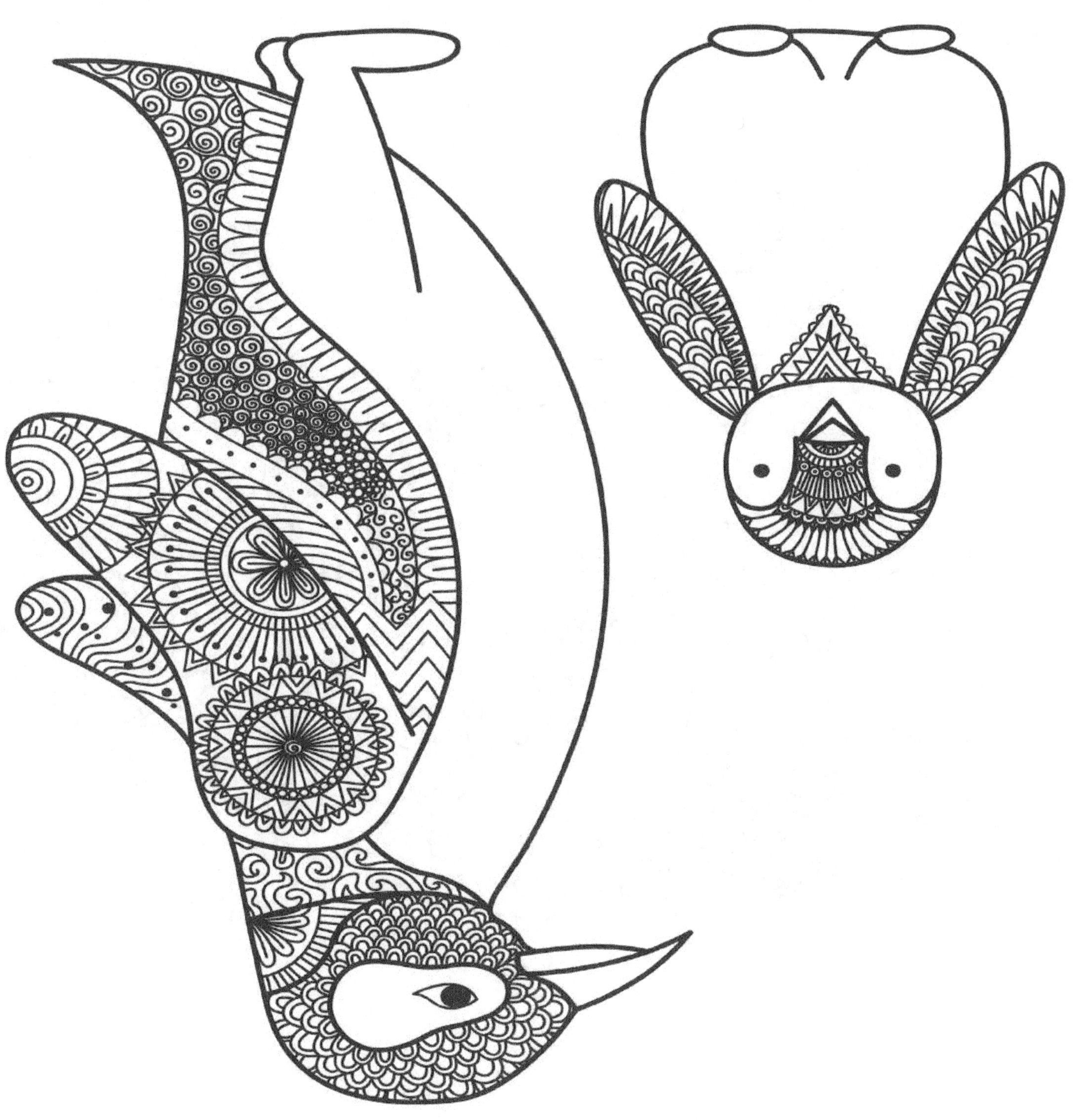